THE GEORGIA POETRY PRIZE

The University of Georgia Press established the Georgia Poetry Prize in 2016 in partnership with the Georgia Institute of Technology, Georgia State University, and the University of Georgia. The prize is supported by the Bruce and Georgia McEver Fund for the Arts and Environment.

SOFT APOCALYPSE

SOFT APOCALYPSE

Leah Nieboer

THE UNIVERSITY OF GEORGIA PRESS

ATHENS

Published by the University of Georgia Press
Athens, Georgia 30602
www.ugapress.org
© 2023 by Leah Nieboer
All rights reserved
Designed by Rebecca A. Norton
Set in Electra LT Std 9.5/20

Most University of Georgia Press titles are
available from popular e-book vendors.

Printed digitally

Library of Congress Cataloging-in-Publication Data
Names: Nieboer, Leah, author.
Title: Soft apocalypse / Leah Nieboer.
Description: Athens : The University of Georgia Press, [2023] |
Series: The Georgia Poetry Prize | Includes bibliographical references.
Identifiers: LCCN 2022043817 (print) | LCCN 2022043818 (ebook) |
ISBN 9780820363691 (trade paperback) | ISBN 9780820363707 (ebook) | ISBN
9780820363714 (pdf)
Subjects: LCGFT: Poetry.
Classification: LCC PS3614.I3549 S64 2023 (print) |
LCC PS3614.I3549 (ebook) | DDC 811/.6—dc23/eng/20220921
LC record available at https://lccn.loc.gov/2022043817

LC ebook record available at https://lccn.loc.gov/2022043818

for my friends, dreamers all

CONTENTS

ONLY IN MY NIGHTS DID THE WORLD
SLOWLY REVOLVE. Halogen drop in the spokes. I
reached through and, on one side, a hard tiredness overtook
me, on the other, the moon shouldered off its clouds, took
what it was offered. A job as an understudy, a flower from the
hardware store, a nickel for example is easy. *I am also other
than what I imagine myself to be.* . . . A diorama of the room
affords only a secondhand sofa, a proposal (juked), a view of all
those happy girls pressed up against the walls in the violeted
light. *I'm yours, too, Anonymously—*

MINOR EVENTS 1

between atoms the implausible cosmonaut

in her heart-shaped sunglasses

in her slick ruby suit

turns herself slowly into

the chlorinated blue

belonging to the public pool

as if every event

announces strange beloveds

nearly naked swimmers

avoid her slipstream—

they point to the shimmering belly

as it turns up

it wants to be licked

the sun does it

the radio static

the slice of a skateboard

behind the fence—

in the beginning there was

the navel

a striated color

something rising between

her legs—

the trajectory became

elliptical—

in the movies

people are lonely and kissing

their worlds together

in the next scene

one girl rotates under

another girl

saying *yes*

like or unlike this

absurd person

a minor event

in the water

here is the angel

wants to drag her under

ANGEL OF MEMPHIS

I am driving west

into the dust devils of

my Oklahoma mind,

my Amarillo, Texas

fictions—

my dreams in the house

not ours

in New Mexico—

I'd like to be as young as the rain

as unashamed as a trumpet

the lick

coaxing itself down

forever

a stumbling blue alley

for what

for whoever's

I guess

loose change

some machines

are whirring on early
outside my window
this morning
by the sound of it
are nearly broke down
though who knows

I'm not working them

I could be dreaming them

their perfected limbs
not seized up
like a throat
like this

a set of knuckles

its fisted fortunes

dropped rushed rushing

in the gutter oh

your face

from here is

escaping

still

GUSTY WINDS MAY EXIST. dust storms the next five miles—I'd made sacrifices, nova in the envelope of my chest. I refused to participate in ultimate events. soaped up each morning thanking the cicadas coming wet and silent out of their shells . . . one year I wrote love letters, 156, to complete strangers then abruptly gave them up. rolled away from the exponential, passed the sex shop glowing over my face, me, like some fated foil in a triple-X rock opera—*it was, after all, my moment!* the stitch of a film frame blitzing out an illness, a lyric complication, shit fiction. I dreamt myself out of bed. the insomniac choir overhead went on buzzing up a line of credits.

FLASH PROCESSING OF A PRIVATE YEAR

wholly spent it seems

standing in a fluorescent line

at the pharmacy

a depression behind the auricular

function *fissure window—Next*

hacking the deathquiet of

the alphabet

spiraling in a weather

an acidic rain slants

anachronic traveling her

spine.

where environment where

incidental *sorry* collisions key up

the uneasy cosmology

into public disarrangement.

make a run for it, Listener—

the clavicle punctures up

the nerves articulate the back of

the heart doing its best

stalling the mean angular motion of

stratum her body flinty

the body an event eventual

everybody open and fantasizing

in collapsing fashion

a stellar and maybe arthritic

sweet Lord, Hail Mary rhetoric

trying to pray praying

over cold coffee

the runtime spooling out

over the counter

cross-referencing herself in

keystrokes drum rattle

a handful of

lifecycles crumpled receipts

saved up

against the atomic clock—

velocity escapes—

the mouth the mouth full of

hopelessly tangled cassette tape.

a strip of numerical detachments

a woman leans across

slips

a bright pink pill

just like the kiss of

an answer

into her palm *well*

we all need a little help sometimes

baby a torn off glorious color

her voice

calling up a cold sweat

a dance floor

a kind of prayer spinning its

glittering record inside of *what*

an unfeeling sentence

the official measure of

a complete and undeviating

orbital oranging everybody

this is the year baby

lashing against

the backward infliction of

the epic the beatific

idea the body shimmies out of

making a passionate making

micrometrical escapes

toward the zerostream's

barely audible pulmonics

intimating *will you call me*

can you let me know if

the books fall off the shelves

like synchronized swimmers

their spines coming apart

underwater the protective envelope

dissipates shining weightless

not trying to be good after all

they only use the word containment

or was it contaminant

after somethings *(well many somethings)*

spilled

guttering somewhere

inside her voice her

vocables pitching over

a string of untenable letters

pulled loose loosening

will you let me know if

the pressure's alright you're alright or

too much

function a fissure her

fisting the crisp sheets

the shape

thrown back with a hard

swallow —

will you let me know —

her hip digging into

the cold metal table

like a joke

splitting the room

then running

out of reach *oh*

sorry

incidentals

purpling up

the harmless marvel of

her thigh.

sirens going off

outside testing the sky's

civically held

breath

cyan and shallow

like a basin for ritual

whose hands

terror error push collect

remember her

softbound recursive *push overflow*

ON A SLEEPLESS NIGHT, KILOMETERS AND
KILOMETERS BELOW WHAT HAD BEEN A
GREAT CITY, we go on our knees to the church of the neon
cross, watch supplicants race the strip, no muffler, smoke tearing
through our nostrils, pink Jesus blinking mutely overhead in a
final effort to turn our eyes up from the buckled pavement—
at what price? *you're still the person I wanted to tell about the
changes I've been making.* we trade between our emptied hands.
we look again at the disaster, we mark each other, semantic
insecurity, *at what point does a person become sad and solitary?*
is a question Lispector never answered after a long drag on her
cigarette.

in the soft underside of the ashen city, I dream we've written
the end of the movie. I wake up and find we've written only
how do I get out of this production machine.

MINOR EVENTS 2

when I got older

I went to parties

people dressed and undressed

like cosmonauts

they blew smoke into each other's

mouths little crises

I had a crush

on everybody

the way they pitched tents

in their speaking

eased open the flaps

climbed inside

silvered them up laughing

while they did it

how they did it

was a secret

so casual

what rolled under and under

their faces

something sticky on top

every surface was phantasmic

the kitchen was

cosmically dirty

I bet the couch was dirty

anyway I sat on it

twisting a paper wrapper

talking a buzzed up hour

with a friend

we passed it back and forth

there was a distance

we kept it

someone was watching us

I learned later

I was mostly sober then

when I got older

a private explorer

I wasn't so careful

I swam to the edge

of a dazzling pool

it was so chic

it was so clean

a man invited me

I wore hardly anything

a little blue

he took a picture

he deleted it later

never got in the water

sat above me on the ledge just

dipped his fingers in

OR WAS LIVING LIKE A SLEEPWALKER THE
GREATEST ACT OF TRUST? January light on the stair.
I've walked at least a hundred years to their ashtray ends in a
drainage ditch, a plastic baggie, a crumpled back alley, or here,
the parking lot of the Blue Sparrow, a handful of quarters in
the meter, *o vacancy !* the last time we were together you
could not look me in the eye. an accident guttering outside the
barred windows, chrome angels coming through the walls for
me—*only I will know.* a soft girl leaning away. figures in the
anemic glow.

*I LET HER GO ON LET US RUMBLE IN THE
FOG* . . . *fell in love, fell in love, fell in love.* a thrifted arrangement. I cross by chain-link fences, their guard dogs, abandoned Christmas lights, the multicolored ones, black cats slipping through the holes . . . somebody is leaning against a doorframe, somebody is playing dominoes in plastic lawn chairs, a cigarette hanging off their lips. I pass the house breaking apart at the edge of my dreams. *we begin from the ruin we helped cause,* I think, but who isn't going around here with a name or two sewn to their chests, right there, *honey* out in the open.

THIS WAS AFTER MIDNIGHT AT THE CORNER STORE

and summer was a slow idea barely

coming around sleepless someone

had called an ambulance

causing a sorrow to appear

on the pavement

a stubborn flower ragged

a silk breath asking

any animal

preferably a tiger to appear

to slip down the cold aisles

to eat all of this

crinkled up *everything*

is contemporary of the present

blue lights sweeping our hair

back off our foreheads I wish it were

a decade ago

an old boyfriend could be

running across a street careless

in his pin-striped valet vest stealing through

the shined cars the traffic my heart nearly

stopped in the air horses

not what I wanted

phantasmic colors stepping across

the tops of the buildings easily

watercolor horses changing

the lights a mirror a conveyer belt

a little wet pushing a cold soda

me shuffling along someone else

scanning up and down for what

all this time alone sleepless might

be worth anyway someone

is slamming tender on the counter

is calling an ambulance

we don't think we are prepared

for death and by strangers like this

arms full of paper bags

I fell back into unbalanced

a little embarrassed *it's okay really it's*

okay—

RELEASED FROM THE NECESSITY OF APOLOGY, we are facing the scrim wall, it is a very bright Sunday morning we've come to: bare feet leaving rhythmic traces in the torn light, voices driven to the remotest corner of the room. *I'm not claiming I'm pure.* a sleepless night always leaves me in a stupor. a throttle of subway cars, unforeseen delays, loose change, a future taped haphazardly to the back of my heart. *we simply got older . . .*

a blueprint for a new October, amoebic beehive in the brain. *variation is not the same as rolling away but each love wants to be the only compromise of its kind.*

unquestioned,

pressed and ready, I lace up an incantation at the door and
follow a loop of desire down the sidewalk, kicked along by
doubt and by epiphany. her leftover night makes distortions
of—*was it you this time—was it me—*

DREAM OF RISKED PHRASES IN SPACE

failing spectacularly at orderliness the primroses

rush hour yellowness

a soft geometry unfinishing

the edges the sentence

giving in to its most

we could say phosphenic

sense pressure tiny implosions

even in suppose a vacant lot

under terrible conditions the blooms

how they fall together

and fall apart easily

making a damp room

in my ear

the whirr of the fan against

the window against which

in late June we leaned

passing mute fireworks

between us—clinical slingshots

wheeling in the sky—

and heat lighting too

making brief incredible shapes

our hands

not keeping time keeping alternately

the oscilloscope pressed to the roof

of our mouths

their pink apprehensions

unmaking us making us

so possible I believe our lingering

here over and over

rubbing against somehow

what cold and sugarless happens

GOD IS NOT PRETTY. so familiar, sweat-covered, half-dressed, and banging open a screen in the side of a yellow, dirt-encrusted trailer. *what is it that you need,* they said. I said, *not a damn thing.* I handed my hell through the window, not speaking, lips of sand whispering a change in the making, *for better or for worse?* no telling what devils are behind and before us. they turn to stir a pot of beans, mutter something to a figure in the bedsheets, . . . *make you a little change.* nothing adds itself up in the break. I come away with cold coffee, a snake plant, anesthesia for the loving, and a stack of postcards from places I've never been. chemical distortion hits the eye's horizon as the bright planets go up in smoke.

FORECLOSE ME

in this scene a gale blows and scatters my papers

into a profound disorder

then it's the future

                                                a hand rapped on the table

then whatever

the day behind us becomes

a darkened face

an overstuffed letterbox

so sexual or

no one home

at night

a spliced montage of

stolen   split-level dreams

of houses

sleep horses

with time

the desired body will

if you put a little change

in this machine

disappear

quarter after quarter

the hands know what to do

they connect the wires

they plug into the question

the EKG going off

on a little television

in no one's bedroom

four channels tuned

to a purpler future

so what

I deal in raw materials

I deal in dream residuals

I'm not interested

in spending a day

shopping on some avenue

walking an old logic   marvelous rock

on a leash

down the street—

I'm afraid of

the pointing

the abstraction

getting mortgaged

being drug along for   no reason

                 kiss me again

                 kiss me

                 kiss me again

the sun glancing off the cement—

the mouth tastes of zinc—

as it happens

I have always believed

in the baptismal properties

of yellow

in the way violet

fucks pink into purple

       a big promise

       a little change

something

falling from your hand

anyway it's cheap

the proposal

drops like a cardboard set

to the stage

I freeze

everyone watching

everyone made ridiculous

playing a part

the windows blasted open

    a house vaporising behind

    each face as if

we were waking up to something

a short circuit in the weather

my breath on the mirror

after a shower I wouldn't share

      the curtain closes

      on the bed

there is never any time

to return

like a believer

like an earthling *oblivious*

to someone

to this rock

imagine

waking up again

to an unabstracted given

to that canary yellow kitchen

plunging the hands in

the sink flowing over

in retrospect how did I

keep that color

I let it get away with me

I let it wash me out

cycle after cycle

the players are identical

sugarstruck animals

strip after strip after strip

I mean

look at all of this

stupid disturbance

on stained paper

taped to the walls

you photogenic rampant person

December begins to look

like a dream

and someone in the rhythm

who escapes the measure

or only an idea

I harnessed once

for a minute

the love scene was ecstatic

full of believers

October November December

I couldn't go there with you—

I could only go there with you—

I never in the actual

pass through that old house anymore—

I draw big diagrams

I scribble approximations of the future

you'll be a danger forever

to me

ten years is nothing

a little change

a logic of whispers

I'm telling you

there is never any time

you are nobody's church

we are more and more cities

with a steep interval between

delicacies, nothing

we never return to

WASHED-UP ULTRAVIOLET MORNING

in bed in a fever

giving thought to distances

cold little gasps of

misinformation going around

the objects on the nightstand

just the usual

instruments rubbing

together against expression —

we could try a different position.

let the face produce an impression —

a visible crease

articulating the cheek.

in my dream you twined together

an edible flower

its round leaves

a buttery orange

expression of

nasturtium.

a good love

spiraled in.

giving no thought —

we moved

in the reverberation of

the jetstream

the body

glitzing its confetti

hopelessly

across North America —

anything is possible.

anything is possible —

if there were a place

to draw one continuous line

against another—

this could be it,

us folding each other up

at the corners

indicators of future occurrences

and in the center

microchemical raptures

softly ceasing

to be directional—

being dimensional instead—

*I WAS GATHERING RAW MATERIAL, I was
seeking an expanse,* we were living yet at angles to ourselves,
blinking on and off, reversing inside, painting the yellow lines,
the factory floor, the road narrowing, I thought of the space
between my legs, gradients, the fervid rooms, vectors, a rover
powering down, the nearness of my mind to a bird climbing
high and alone in the clear air—*THIS IS A TEST.* the morning
blares its lament over the shifting streets, foreclosures, busted-
up tennis courts I might have used in childhood to practice
my crossover. a future came fast. faster, through the intestines,
heart, liver, cellular transfer, chemical tentacles in the water,
a hiccup in the brain. *at point zero every element becomes a
startling thing.* a wreck becomes an opening, a slick young
porpoise washes up to the sandy edge.

MINOR EVENTS 3

your other ear can be held against me.
— ROSMARIE.WALDROP

an argument is rising through the roof

I'm spaced out listening

to the couple next door

on the upper edge of love, or something

lifting off—

I could it seems

skate the length of these powerlines

to Ophiuchus, taking care

not to trip on a constellation of sneakers

dangling where

the others had thrown them off

I believe in love

in the prayers crossing up

this completest dark

the buzzards on the ridgepole

the flowers coming through the frost

somewhere else

the sun is rising

is shaking through the blinds

my grandfather

in my grandmother's room

is singing

this is only one world

I do remember

opening the valves *dolce, viola,*

vox humana all at once

at the pump organ, hers,

my bare feet

the felt pedals

WE ARE THE ONES THAT SWIM, not diurnal, mechanical, a glass in the hand, honeysuckle, violet eons, slipping the grasp—

love needs reality. the corner store goes out of business after all, the desert moves to the back of the retina, the throat, the glass crushed across the pink tile floor, the stair, the edge of the law catches us, here's a tear

in the dress, the surface, a break in the logic of it, we glitter

softly out of it, half-naked, making an entrance at the abyssal zone—

everyone applauded. *yes,*

everyone it appeared was having a great time. a big, plush-covered expression, a little swizzle around the waists, a place for stretching out

in the middle of what we knew, an excess, a wobble

in each corner, the mismatched confessionals going over and over,
the fringe material sliding up in the low lights—

we turn at the point of entry, idling inside, the room's minor
apprehensions skirting us, just glossing our shifting *in lieu of hope*
back and forth on the soles of the foot then *you*

dear almost impossible

you made an appearance after all, a bright silver, linking herself in
time through us saying—*you're the bottom of the ocean, I'm a fish in
the sky.* we eased ourselves into an open frequency putting the fish
back to water all night.

DREAM OF A SENSIBLE FACTORY

there are exquisite breaks for languishing without reason

in each doorway, *an eccentricity,* a ritual swing

of hours, the variable wash

of light, of the living—

in the factory, it isn't loud, anyone could talk themselves into

a surprise, a purplish exchange, anyone could get a little

dirty, get a little cheeky, *stay awhile please stay*

alive. here everything

is bright. we the workers becoming solar

array, we sit mending this or that

on plush benches in hyperbolic arrangement

sipping a crisp feeling when it's warm

and speculating about

the latest news with an old, amorous

dog at our feet licking them

senseless. clean air

works through
our lungs, clearing the effects of
some man
who appeared on the television in a previous sort
of suit, in a previous sort
of age. we age, we stow our dreams
in our experimental pockets

we finger their edges,
remainders of

the work, ideas, grand jetés, a future of
unsold goods, us—
in each case

they are safe and accessible. we are the ones

who make a riot

of color. someone unthinkable

takes someone's unthinkable hand, carefully

folded, unfolded, we move at different speeds,

arthritis is not a prohibitive condition

for getting paid. *I too*

fold the body into others. it makes a necessary question, it hurts

to ask it and we ask it, we ask it—

this is a soulful operation, we sift ourselves through

its expressions, we let

others come to be.

to be understood, we practice inflating and deflating the lungs

in synchronized fashion, our labor

furling, coming together

extralinguistically—

you can find us

on the hottest day of the year
under the influence of Venus, swimming
without order, sweat on the upper lip, *we observe*
the going world and no figure appears

summarizable, lusty. curiosity loops itself
between our legs, and afterward

the tone is flexible, *meteoric,* we return, we make
fortunate exchanges, cheap toolkits
for heartbreak, unplanned catastrophe, STDs, bad dreams,
no body is an impossible
body, we stitch it into the soft clasp

before sending the materials
to the middles and the borders, to the northern edge
of a city mid-composition—
it's all so fucked, we say to each other—

and *keep going*—

we send sound waves, a kiss, a compass, a forward oscillation
into the desert like a love letter
to the animal, to the person shining up
to a crossing,
to someone's mother still alive watching Jeopardy
in her armchair looking for *just a pinch of*
relief—

the difference between dying and loving is slight—

the world continues almost

entirely at our expense, we send wet dreams down crowded alleyways
of sleeping bags, transparent ceilings
arching up, becoming cathedral,
we toss wreaths around the absences,

jimmy another space out of a resounding

no,

nowhere, somewhere, over and over

perhaps—

when someone dies in the factory, today,

it is without fear. we carry them

off the dance floor, in the discoed light, *in their exuberant whirl*

we send them from our horizon in a bright blue robe

made by hand, studiously sequined, *this is how*

we will recall the time, and what it could have meant

when we slip out of its pocket

when they come smooth and rivering

to gather us remainders in

THINGS HAD GONE BACK TO BEING WHAT THEY WERE. a couple rocking across the television, the scratch of the needle on a worn-out record—*if I were trying to get to Tuskegee, what exit would I take?* another accident flagged on the shoulder, a line of cool-eyed Madonnas at the roadside market, had I left a little lipstick on the pillow, we had left a surgical silence, a tear in the vertical.—*warm me up*

instead with your guesses, dumb suggestions, the truth loops itself out of eyeshot a million miles below the interstate. the years. *go and go*—before I could say what was real and what had gone galloping through my dreams . . . I did get to where I was going next, I stood on a roof half-dressed watching a jet wake stretch itself into the most insane blue you'll ever in sunlight see.

HOWEVER OUT OF ORDER THE BODY IS A
PUBLIC PLACE if only somebody will listen to it—

the rumble of certain cellular exchanges,

siren of its soft tissues,

helicopter whirr as it turns over, *dear insomnia,*

the hanging dial tone of its

most mesopelagic, scattered, fished-for, researched, thieving,
used-up, obstructed

pulses

supplicating at a payphone around the corner, a hiccup, no quarters

for a connection, *hello! hello! hell-O! . . .*

also if people won't.

a building collapses in a foreclosed part of the city and nobody
calls it in, nobody calls to say, "I miss you, green shutters,"
"oh I need you, broken screen door." the bougainvillea grows
bright and long and lazy over the porch—

and an afternoon secretly recorded *like those temporary beds
we made* tangles itself between the vines—gets off—

this isn't about loss,

not exactly, though only readiness is in the end affordable.
she unzips the overnight bag she's always kept in a corner,
ridiculous, she's spilled again into the street, nearsighted,
adjusting, where a developer in slick, camel-colored loafers
appraises the site of each failure eyeing a new upward trajectory
through which the body inevitably falls

quiet.

WHICH IS A SURREPTITIOUS LINE—between two notes of music? there are streetlights, night repairs, there is a little soup, a subrational argument, a discarded silhouette. on side B, someone is raising the rent. black car cruising the windows on the other side of the street where I also am, almost turning inside of that crushed velvet dress—*Happy Christmas,* you texted. quick heavy snow punching a hole in the sky I'll sew up later tonight with old sequins. down at the American Legion, Angel slides a bright green shot down the bar—*honey, don't you know by now? you can play a shoestring so long as you're sincere.*

SPACE WITHOUT MAP

each performance in this lightwashed place

is indecent

a little bruised up nonetheless

prettyish event

        at the back of nowhere

        an accident

here the desert the taxidermist's

church Big Al's Autobody

the honkytonk elementary

school nuclear facility hospital *warning*

the actor gets lifted

then twirls herself billowing

out of reach

in a backless dress

against the defaced shimmering

curb light post fence—

                nothing *drumming*

                under the wheels—

perhaps I am misremembering

the place   *the angel*

                         the interior deployed

the way

        six or so onlookers

        some laughter sirens

        stumbled out of tune

        skirting an orchestral drop

        a crumpled up

        face bag plastic discarded

        etcetera

        out of someone's

        shallow pocket

        in the weeds —

someone's forgotten something

important—

       the hour bows down

       a body bends to the curve

exceeding the function

the sound of

the moment slips

lucid and mute

       accidentally

       out of the moment—

it's important to me

to memorize one's own

temporary address, a clatter

without insurance—

        and the body which lets itself—

looking aslant

        a long slide on the slick

        pavement, glass

        in the notes

an attempt

to wipe the pathos

        the strangers—

from the scene—

        mascara—

        running—

beyond the ear

someone articulates a jeté

from nothing,

`   *there is an abrupt*

                     sound, a cemented ending, a

splash of piss in the alley

where something is always yet

rutting around —

        many people

exist,

I do

well I did once

announce a baptism at this

and a wet trail dribbled quietly

down the sidewalk—

you have come finally

    to the right place,

    Stranger—

    the takeout window slams open

    at the tinny sound of a bell—

    another ticket is stabbed through

    a metal skewer—

    though we hardly know

    how to call

    what this place is—

    a dial tone hanging

    somewhere

    waylaid, interrupted,—

it's so expensive,

the men, their unavoidable orders

on the television

in the locked-up

> *do not disturb*

rooms

the rented arrangements

one after another

cool dispossession

in the right company

which this

isn't, —

before the accident

        at the very beginning

        in the wider aperture of

what happened

before the doorway of that

sequined back alley

somewhere—

      there was a silk dress opening,

        umber, excessive, a murmur

I swear it—

      there was a little rain

      inside the rain

      something shining off

an expectant face

light, rhythmic, authentic

something viscous slipping

from someone's

wide-brimmed hat,

a dress parting

at my back

a little brush of

speculative matter—

no matter—

the long slide on someone's

slick, forgiving

thigh—

grief is mostly private

and I'm not an actor

I was only reaching then

for the stranger

for a rub of her future

like an unmarked rest

in the measure

of the hands

in the moment—

I'd had enough

of the moment—

                    it collapsed me

inside another version

perhaps

I am someone excessively

agreeable free and lucky

a soft apocalypse

I did end that night

aslant in the shimmering

back of a stretch limousine

with a couple of

gorgeous people —

we were giving ourselves someplace

to go —

                 here —

we were here giving each other

explicit reasons

to go on

NOTES

Most prose poems borrow their initial lines from Clarice Lispector's *The Passion According to G.H.*, translated by Alison Entrekin.

Some of the angels and strange beloveds wouldn't exist without Rainer Maria Rilke's *Duino Elegies*, especially "The First Elegy," in which he writes, "Weren't you always / distracted by expectation, as if every event / announced a beloved?"

"*ONLY IN MY NIGHTS DID THE WORLD SLOWLY REVOLVE*" borrows the phrase "a nickel is easy" from William Gass's "Gertude Stein and The Geography of the Sentence: Tender Buttons." I stole the speculative possibility in "I am also other than [what] I imagine myself to be" from Simone Weil's *Gravity & Grace*.

The bird "high and alone in the clear air" in "*I WAS GATHERING RAW MATERIAL*" also appears in Simone Weil's *Gravity & Grace*.

"MINOR EVENTS 3" is for Antje (Ann) Apotheker Nieboer (August 4, 1936–October 10, 2020) and Nicolas Nieboer.

The question put to Lispector in "*ON A SLEEPLESS NIGHT, KILOMETERS AND KILOMETERS BELOW WHAT HAD BEEN A GREAT CITY*" comes from a 1977 interview aired on *Fundação Padre Anchieta (TV Cultura)*.

The soft girl leaning in and out of "*OR WAS LIVING LIKE A SLEEPWALKER THE GREATEST ACT OF TRUST?*" is an echo from Hillary Gravendyk's *The Soluble Hour*.

"*RELEASED FROM THE NECESSITY OF APOLOGY*" borrows the phrase "we are facing the scrim wall" and its bright Sunday morning from James Baldwin's *The Amen Corner.*

The primroses in "DREAM OF RISKED PHRASES IN SPACE" are transplanted from Bernice Van Gorp's garden, where I've spent many imaginative hours.

The first line of "FORECLOSE ME" re-visions a sentence from Lispector's *The Passion According to G.H.* The hand rapping on the table is taken from Samuel Beckett's *Ohio Impromptu.* The idea of violet fucking pink into purple is Derek Jarman's, from "Purple Passage," *Chroma.*

"*You can play a shoestring if you're sincere*" is something John Coltrane said once, and which I have remixed, repeated, or misremembered often—here, as the final phrase in "*WHICH IS A SURREPTITIOUS LINE.*"

The materials that compose "DREAM OF A SENSIBLE FACTORY" were collected across numerous cities and homes over the past few years: the "*world [that] continues almost entirely at our expense,*" from *Vertigo* by Joanna Walsh; various desires, dreams, excesses, and pluralities made in friendship with others, our murmured conversations, especially those in Denver; former lovers; the dog I borrowed for a few hours one winter; though the "exuberant whirl" belongs particularly to José Esteban Muñoz (*Cruising Utopia*), the resounding to the *tympanum* of the ear, the hyperbolic space to the ocean.

"SPACE WITHOUT MAP" invokes "the hour bows down" from Rilke's *The Book of Hours* and includes traces of uncountable others.

ACKNOWLEDGMENTS

My immense gratitude goes to Andrew Zawacki for selecting and believing in this book. I am also grateful to Bethany Snead, Elizabeth Adams, Lea Johnson, and the staff at the University of Georgia Press.

Thank you to Blas Falconer for selecting "FLASH PROCESSING OF A PRIVATE YEAR" for the 2022 Mountain West Writers' Contest and *Western Humanities Review* for publishing it.

To Graham Foust, Bin Ramke, and Selah Saterstrom for being readers of these poems.

To Joanna Szachowska, whose oneiric work in the high desert resonated with me on gut and spirit levels and whose "Playing with Fire" now covers these poems. Thank you for making this possible. To possible worlds —

For the robust and continuous support of my writing life, thank you to my extended family from The MFA Program for Writers at Warren Wilson College.

For your friendship — and the belief, support, joy, intelligence, and possibility you offered, which has made me, and the making of this particular book, possible — thank you to Sally Keith, Hannah Peet, Katherine and Rob Rooks and family, Kathleen and Reed Turchi, Meghan and Nate Williams, RJ Bracchitta, Becky Fink, Tariq Luthun, Megan Pinto, Robert Matt Taylor, my brothers and sister-in-law, Jesse, Micah, and Leah (Engelbrecht) Nieboer, Lauren Dent and Jonathan Coe, Sam Barber, Stella Corso, Patrick Cottrell, Cass Eddington, Joanna Howard, Ella Longpre, Leia Lynn, Lucien Meadows, Madison Myers, Aleks Prigozhin, Bin, twice over, Alex Toy, and Anna Zumbahlen.

THE GEORGIA POETRY PRIZE

Christopher Salerno, *Sun & Urn*

Christopher P. Collins, *My American Night*

Rosa Lane, *Chouteau's Chalk*

Chelsea Dingman, *Through a Small Ghost*

Chioma Urama, *A Body of Water*

Jasmine Elizabeth Smith, *South Flight*

Leah Nieboer, *Soft Apocalypse*

Printed in the USA
CPSIA information can be obtained
at www.ICGtesting.com
LVHW040156071023
760365LV00004B/483

9 780820 363691